WORDS FROM MY HEAD
A collection of poems

BY SIMON MATHIS

ISBN: 979-8-218-60345-8

DEDICATION

For Paul, Merlin & Tallulah
My hearth, my heart, my home

CONTENTS

40th Birthday Portrait of Simon Mathis by Zachary Ares, 2022, photographed by Simon Mathis, 2022, cropped. Both Copyright © 2022, Simon James Mathis.

Preface

For a collection of poems from an unknown poet to exist without a preface seems incomplete somehow. Although, I know that I usually skip over this part of most books to get to what is actually going on inside. However, whether you are here because you are the type of person to read a book from cover to cover, or if you have actually read some or all of these poems and want to understand a little bit more about what got me here and why, then you are very welcome. For those people who will never read this, that's more than ok too, I'll never know and neither will you.

As a former dancer, for me poetry is a choreography of language. The opportunity to let words and the thoughts they contain start and stop, twist and turn, and jump and roll. In essence, making words dance on the page is delightful to me. Using the musicality and rhythm that is available to express, emphasize and extend my thoughts and feelings can feel like creating magic spells at times and my mind dances because of it. Most of my poems have rhymes within them, not because I believe that rhymes are necessary for poetry and not because I cannot create without them but purely because I enjoy them. Enjoyment was the purpose behind them.

These poems have been written over the past decade or so for no other reason than I felt a need to write them. Sometimes, I've had periods of intense poetry writing that produce a lot of material and sometimes one single idea, feeling or moment will strike me. They are an expression of thoughts that were rattling from side to side in my head and also an avenue by which to process them. They fed a need for creativity within the moment and to set them down was to set them free. After releasing and capturing a poem, I felt a sense of relief that I cannot fully define but it has helped me by being a sort of lightning rod for my emotions. Usually, after I have written a poem, I don't return to the substance of it but on review I do sometimes tinker around with the odd word and with the punctuation. The punctuation is there to aid understanding, for clarity and sometimes rhythm. I hope the decoration of full-stops (periods), commers, exclamation points etc., help, rather than hinder you as you read on.

Overall, these poems were created for my own private reflections. A few have been shared with friends and family for their consideration and only once have I stood up and delivered a public reading. I do have a purpose behind why I have chosen to self-publish these but for now that purpose remains private. To make them easier to read, I've divided them into four sections, Power, Nature, People and Dark Days. Then arranged them in a way that I feel has flow, in case you are brave enough to read from one to the next. However, that was just in the compilation process and not the writing experience. Many of these poems, I enjoy revisiting time and again. Whereas others I find myself challenged by, either because I don't want to revisit the moment or mood or because I am not entirely happy with the outcome. However, I wrote them with a purpose and perhaps it is no longer for me but might be for someone else. I have a second book of poetry that I conceived as a collection. It is still in the works, and maybe, one day I will complete it.

Simon, January 2025

Poems of Power

WORDS FROM MY HEAD

I shall make a magic

I shall make a magic and roll it in my hands,
I shall breathe with little puffs and feel as it expands.
I shall pull a golden ball and feel it gently grow,
And taste the light that I can see, and sense and feel
      and know.

I shall make a magic and hold it at my heart,
I shall guard its gentle light, its bigger little part.
I shall keep its secret now and cherish it with love
And wrap it freely with my soul, entwined below
      above.

I shall make a magic when I am at peace,
I shall guide a part of me to gradually increase.
I shall grow and know some more until I really see
Just what it is and how it works and when to set it free

I shall make a magic and let it flow around,
I shall leave it room to move, to fly and float and
      ground.
I shall let it crackle now and spark and fizz for me
Until such time I find some sense unveiled of mystery.

Still Moving

Stop a while
Pause your body
Still a moment
Hold your breath

Freeze your movement
Wait in situ
Halt momentum
Suspend death

Listen closely
Feel your body
Pumping blood out
From your heart

Pounding eardrums
Lungs are bursting
Gasping intake
Now restart

For Fuck's Sake

For Fuck's sake just be beautiful because you really are.
Take a look and find one thing you like and hold that star.
A shining thing, a guiding light, a place from which to start
To find more stars and navigate and heal your wounded
     heart.

For Fuck's sake just go easy on yourself and what you do.
Perfection isn't all that great and perfect limits you.
So be a little messy and then be a mess a lot.
Creation comes from who you are, it isn't who you're not.

For Fuck's sake just be beautiful because it's really true.
It doesn't matter what the noise keeps whispering to you.
Drown out the sounds that drag you down and play a
     different song.
Songs of love and songs hope 'cause here's where you
     belong.

Fortify

Beware of the hero in all their own stories,
Beware of the teller of somebody's tales.
Watch out for the warnings of others' behavior,
When the teller more often that action entails.

Take heed of the way that they treat all the servers,
The waiters, the door-folk, the cab drivers too.
'Cause this is the way they think people are treated
 And one day the person they treat will be you.

Observe when you speak just how much they listen
How much they are thinking and what they take in.
Or are they just planning the next thing they're
        saying?
Who wants you to finish, so they can begin.

Be mindful of people who sit in harsh judgement,
The righteous, the proper, an eye for an eye.
Especially those, when the rules don't include them.
When charity's cold and forgiveness runs dry.

Give sparingly to those same ones who are taking,
And taking and taking, again and again.
Your energy, favors and money and moments,
As nothing will quite fill the void of their drain.

So, fortify yourself from such people,
Who bluster and bolster and bash and barge in.
Surround yourself with people of kindness,
Who love you, support you and want you to win.

I made a mistake and then I died

I made a mistake today and then I died.
All of my embarrassment rose up inside
As I flushed and I blushed, and I stammered and cried.
My outside all crumbled, my inside all cried.
My energy drained and it sank to the floor;
An overreaction that's happened before.
Adrenaline boosted and pumped up some more.
The lights had all gone out, I searched for the door!
Yet I just stood there and smiled serene,
I took a deep breath as I surveyed the scene.
I took a big run up and said what I mean
And nobody noticed the mess I had been.

Humanity Dance

Stories ripple, swimming tails and flashing ends of dreams,
Where memories float and twisting strands entwine in
    silken schemes.
Pages fly and paper trails read black and white in reams,
As ghosts of ghosts remember hosts repeating ancient
    themes.
Forgetting what you didn't know, reminding us again
Of ancient thoughts and older truths of how we will
    remain.
For future selves and lessons learned translated for our
    time
And coded in our souls once more to reenact a mime
Of wisdom waltzing hand in hand, our partner for a day.
Our precious friend glides swiftly through as we re-clear
    the way.
And on it goes and carries through, an essence at the core
Ever thus but changed by us, a little or some more.

Palace Hall

Through corridors and halls we walk
With pictures hanging by.
Tap wooden planks and tiled floors
And windows seeking sky.

Glints of glass and gilded gold
And stone steps spiral high.
Wrought iron scroll and brass handrail
Steps tracing days gone by.

Past fire hearths and candelabra,
Memories of flame,
Where rustled silks and petticoats
Along that ground once came.

And fragrant airs of sweet perfume
May linger just the same
Of forgotten lives and whispered tales
Where only shades remain.

Angled Angel

Blue-eyed lady with sharp edges
Dreams of moments flashing through.
Inspiration, light divining
Auras, colours, golden hue.
Special lady, full of promise
Magic angel, unaware.
Beauty from a reserve hidden
Casting spells and flowing air
Changing times and pausing moments
Reaching for an unknown time.
Placed down now and quite forgotten
Seeking freedom within rhyme.

Passing the Future

The whispered winds of future take us down the paths we
could not know
Into places unforeseen and unimagined where we'd go.
Buffeted through broken feelings, thoughts of who we might
well be
Into places unexpected, shepherded or roaming free.
Gentle paths with undulations, twisting paths that started
straight
Knotted laces loosen fraying, lighter trappings gaining weight.
Experience and deepened furrows, frowns and laughter settle
in
Thickened waistline, weary joints and extra pounds and
sagging skin.
If I knew then what I know now, how my choices would have
changed
But I didn't and I couldn't; life we had won't be exchanged.

The Fool

Sitting on a precipice
Thinking of the world
The winds all blowing round him
Through his life is hurled
Thinking of the past days
Thinking of this time
Thinking of his plans to make
And hoping for a sign

Standing on a precipice
Looking out to sea
The winds all blowing round him
His heart is trapped and free
Remembering some past times
And waiting for the new
And wondering just where to go
And planning what to do

Walking on a precipice
His arms outstretched and wide
The winds all blowing round him
There's nothing he will hide
This place may have its dangers
But the view's so good
And the wind is on his face here
His path he's understood

cont.

Dancing on a precipice
His face turned to the sky
Smiling at the sunshine while the
People point and cry
And they look at him in wonder
Afraid that he might die
Then they see his free abandon
That they know they'll never try

He keeps on

Dancing on a precipice
Just look he's dancing on
To the music from the Heavens
And the Earth's pulsating song
And the winds that blow around him
Lift his arms up high
And the harmonies within his soul
Teach him how to fly

Arias for Angels

On days of noises and traffic and bustle
     of overwhelming riot and fuss,
With the bother of honking horns and people
     being angry people.
Of greys and browns and sludge and slips
     and pushes and shoves and noise and news;
People wail and sirens scream.
     Sirens wail and people scream.
I lift my eyes up to the skies
     and rise and rise and rise.
               I float up and I rise.

Let me go up into the blues,
     away from the mes and away from the yous
Let me go up to the blue skies
     and rise and rise and rise.
Let me float up into the clouds,
     away from the many, away from the crowds
Let me float up to the cloud lands
     and rise and rise and rise.

I feel a colour surround me,
     floating, lifting, whisping through
Turquoise trimmed with ribboned gold,
     older, folded hue
Magic light and iridescence,
     skim a surface quite unseen
To a song that floats up higher,
     peaceful, ceaseful and serene.

cont.

Let me go up into the blues,
    joining the mes and joining the yous
Let me go up to the blue skies
    and rise and rise and rise.
Let me float up into the clouds,
    at one with the many at one with the crowds
Let me float up to the cloud lands
    and rise and rise and rise
        and drift away.

To Come

Think on this, my angel dearest
I would, all your stories told.
If I could see your winding histories;
Many journeys to unfold.

This I wish, to bring you peaceful
Days and nights and years to come.
Fulfilled dreams and heartfelt passions
Successes, loves and battles won.

Fondest love to you my darling,
Hopeful, joy-filled down the years.
And in the end on balance more of
Days of laughter than of tears.

Poems of Nature

Told

Silence settles soundlessly
Waiting weighted will
Ending echoes emptying
Restless reactions resolve
Mindful moments muster
Peaceful pacing plains
Distant drying deserts
Serene submerging seas
Breath beginning being
Value volumes void
Qualities quaintly quelled
Tales telling told

Morning Sun

The morning sun's golden rays
Reach across landscapes
Touching the world

With shards of warmth
Piercing the sleep of night
Rousing dreams of day

Caressing fingers of light
Inspires new plans
Hopes and challenges

Dawn of possibility
Rises above the horizon
Spreading awakening

Visions of tomorrow
Yesterday's goals
Enacted today

Glory lifting high
Reducing cool shadows
Evaporating dew

Creation fed anew
Unique repetition
For this moment

cont.

Time still moving
Still time moving
Moving time still

Time moving still
Toward heat of this day
Unknown, untapped, unsullied

Psp Psp

Psp Psp Psp
With one eye open
Psp Psp Psp
Is watching there
Psp Psp Psp
Is on alert and
Psp Psp Psp
Gone from the chair

Mep Mep Mep
The cupboard open
Mep Mep Mep
All love and care
Mep Mep Mep
I'm under foot now
Mep Mep Mep
My bowl is bare

Psp Psp Psp
Under the bed now
Psp Psp Psp
Retreated there
Psp Psp Psp
Is out of reach with
Psp Psp Psp
Unblinking stare

cont.

Mep Mep Mep
With tail a quiver
Mep Mep mep
I see you there
Mep Mep Mep
I want to play now
Mep Mep Mep
All fluff and hair

Psp Psp Psp
Is so well hidden
Psp Psp Psp
Ensconced somewhere
Psp Psp Psp
We try to find her
Psp Psp Psp
Retreated there

Mep Mep Mep
Of friendly greeting
Mep Mep Mep
Cause you went where?
Mep Mep Mep
You went and left me
Mep Mep Mep
I'm glad you're there

End of a long day

Dying embers, sacred light
Tired day and weary night
Beaten track and tearing thorns
Through the fog as black crow mourns.
Climbing day and weary mind
Searching long and never find
Briars of repeated task.
Body fights 'gainst what I ask.
Tired day and weary mind
Twisting paths, cruel and unkind
With blurry smoke in teary eyes
Heavy heart and weary sighs.
Longing for some sleeping spell
Dreamless, lightless, resting knell.

Shadows

Shadows gather all around me
Creeping through the unmarked way
Settling down in long forgotten
Paths that twist and turn away
Deep I'm lead on cheerless journeys
Down the tracks of yesterday
Avenues of past remembrance
Echoed cries of "come what may"
Weathered stones and faded markers
Tell no more what once they'd say
Hiding truths distorting reason
Keeping darkness far from day

Golden Hues

As autumn starts to draw upon us
Green to yellow mellows through
And now the summer's warmth is over
And the dawns are mist and dew
Now on the trees the leaves are turning
Turning golden, golden hue

As the sharp wind eddies round me
Crisp the leaves now dusting through
And now the sun's long days are over
And it's warming hours few
There in the field the leaves are turning
Turning golden, golden hue

As the palate now is changing
Red, orange, yellow, browns come through
And greens give way to mellow over
And new is old when old is new
When in my soul the leaves are turning
Turning golden, golden hue

As my love has aged and swollen
Stolen time has travelled through
And now the time of lush green's over
And the days have gone we knew
For in my heart the leaves are turning
Turning golden, golden hue

cont.

Pick some moment make a picture
'fore the winter follows through
And before the autumn's over
Before the final debt is due
Then in my dream the leaves are turning
Turning golden, golden hue

Dark Rains

Peaceful patter of nighttime rainfall
Washes thoughts of the day from me
Fears and failures, unaccomplished
Abject terrored misery
The dark of night and chilling water
Often raises stranger fears
But tonight, the nature's music
Rhythmic stillness in my ears
Drips on tree boughs, sky-borne rivers
Tears of nature flowing free
Releases all my pent-up tension
And allows me just to be

December Moon

Oaken Moon, Cold Moon,
Winter Moon, Wolf Moon.

Winter's edge is full
Darkness spreads its cowl.
Frost bound dead leaves fall,
Ice chill cruel winds howl.
Cold touched dark hands pall,
Old-clutched dreams low growl.

Winter Moon, Colden Moon,
Wolfer Moon, Oaken Moon.

As mounting knots
Of darkness gather round,
With chilling spilling tingle
Down the neck,
Slipping quickened patter
On the ground,
Sensing danger
Keeping nerves in check.

Hurry home hurry on,
Scurry to scurry from,
Count your steps,
Won't be long
Till a light
Means darkness gone.

The First Snow

Whitened lands of winter 'wakens
Dormanting trees loose final leaves
Flash of reds in icing landscapes
Chilling flakes on windy breeze

Duvet snow on fir-tree branches
Silver distant trunks of trees
Grey-blue skies of slatey mornings
Sheltered moment in the lees

Scattering flakes and chilling eddies
Hardened ground and earthly freeze
Solid waters' movements ceasing
First of many days like these

Odocoileus

Cloudy skies hide moon and starlight
Winter's blackness snows remove
Dark and still on silvered landscape
Frozen trees that do not move
Woodlands lay with coldest coating
Bleakest branches trim improve
Odocoileus in the clearing
Lifelessness here to disprove

Antlered head raised on a whisper
Graceful movement sensing near
Icy breath absent while frozen
Twitch ear alert for sound to hear
Distant stalking crunch of footfall
In the snow that ends the year
Quick escape of flashing movement
Fleeting white-tail fleeing fear

Poems of People

The Strawberry Toast

For the people who taste like strawberries
For the people who shine from within
For the people who radiate kindness
For the people who let love begin

For the people who spread calm around them
For the people who sacrifice more
For the people who stare wide in wonder
For the people who open the door

For the people who fetch and they carry
For the people who serve with a smile
For the people who seek out tomorrow
For the people who dream for a while

For the people who rise to the challenge
For the people who fail but don't end
For the people who build and create art
For the people who fix, and they mend

For the people who tell bedtime stories
For the people who read books aloud
For the people who hear music playing
For the people who laugh lots out loud

For the people who see clouds as pictures
For the people who stare at the sea
For the people who look at old photos
For the people who love you and me

Princess Spaceship and the Space Unicorn

"You are Princess Spaceship" Josh declared his sister Eve
"And you shall rule the galaxy, and I will never leave".
"And you are the Space Unicorn" she said with all her might.
Her little brother Josh shook out his mane and said "That's right!"

Then they both jumped on the sofa and they flew off into space.
They flew three times around the moon and spun it out of place.
Then they put the sofa in reverse, and flew three circles back
Cause it's never good to leave a mess and take the moon off track.

They clung on to some cushions as the Princess shouted "Go!"
She hit some dials and buttons and that made the engines glow.
And the Unicorn, he used his horn just like a magic key,
That could fly them where they wanted on the count of "1,2,3".

They had a bumpy landing but they landed all the same
And hand in hand they went to see this new and vast terrain.
While Princess Spaceship led the way, Space Unicorn took the rear
As they went into the dining room they said "We show no fear!"

But could they hear some footsteps coming slowly down the
        stairs?
And will a fearsome monster coming catch them unawares?
They dived under the tablecloth in just the nick of time
Would they be caught here trespassing, an intergalactic crime?

cont.

They huddle close together hearing Space Police alarms.
As mummy lumbered passed them with the laundry in her arms.
They rolled out from the table as Space Unicorn lead the way
They heard a growling bear attack and saying "Oi, you, stay!"

And daddy chased them round the room and made them laugh
    with glee.
And Mummy laughed and chased them saying
      "Time for space aged tea!"

Payment on Account

I hear your gallows humour and the drum beat pounding on
As your heart's mind flickers round the crowding, crowded,
    growling throng
Of the people that you've known and loved now twisting in your
    view.
Into strangers, fogged and hazy, crazed and ravaged. Then for
    who?

I see the man behind you wraps a cowl around your mind;
The warmth and comfort offered of a shallow, dangerous kind.
And all the bones are polished when the flesh has gone away,
As an omen of your future after suffering decay.

Your disguise of noise and colour is distracting and denying
Defence inflates around you of deceiving and defining
But the creature underlying he is shivering and crying
And all the while you're lying to yourself and on the floor.

Please, look in the mirror and then turn up the lights.
Let loving kindness fuel you on and not these dark delights.
Your friends now have to leave you from your sights and all your
    slights.
They're exhausted from your cruelty and you ever needing more.

Try shrugging off the robing, let it fall on to the floor
And be naked in the daylight as you never were before.
Some shadows may seem longer but some demons move
    away.
I pray the terrors of your night-time might announce a
    dawning day.

The stranger you know

You're rushing to get somewhere quickly
Past a man with a case on the stairs,
You chose to be late and to help him
And let your dad knows someone cares.

A little old lady out shopping
As she struggles to get the job done
You get her the box from the high shelf
And look at the face of your mum.

That child who is crying on long haul,
His mother with tears on her face,
You smile and you offer to hold him,
And remember your own son's embrace.

When they sat at the table together
And talked through events of their day
They spoke of some small acts of kindness
From the strangers they met on their way.

This great human race is still running
Towards or away or around
And I'd still rather be in the back half
Than to crush one more face in the ground.

I look at a crowd full of strangers
And see all the people I've known,
I hope that some stranger showed kindness
And stopped them from struggling alone.

In Chorus

It's hard when I remember at the root and at the core
That I feel a little rotten-broken; damaged from before
And that core is clinging on a bit and hasn't gone away
And I carry on and live with it and struggle on each day
Then I walk into a room and everybody starts to sing
And I feel a little better and a little light comes in.

See, all the things we want to be and wished to be and tried
And all the little cuts and scrapes and ways we were denied
They don't disappear for me or go but may retract
When I make a move and come to you, and choose that I
    will act
Then I walk into a room and I can know I'm not alone.
And I feel a little better 'cause the singers makes a home.

It may not be a perfect crowd, we may not all get on
But there's unity and harmony and space within each song.
There's vibration and there's resonance and healing in the
    sound
And there's hope and love and power stirring deep within
    the ground.

And the energy and strength and beat and rhythm all
    around
Is an ever growing future and a wholeness that we've found.
Then we walk out of the room and we can know that we are
    one
'Cause the total of our whole is so much greater than the
    sum.

Golden Boy

Golden boy with golden hair
Deep brown eyes and distant stare
Chest hair swirl like Van Gogh's stars
Sharing tales and talking scars
Naughty schoolboy cheeky grin
Playing games, engaging sin
In my arms and in my mind
Pounding hearts bodies entwinned
Gentle touch and rougher play
Tousled hair and look away
Golden boy hails golden day
Stayed a while then flew away

What?

I don't understand where you come from
I can't understand what you do
I don't see your viewpoint as valid
I think all you think of is you

It matters who kisses which someone?
If a girl likes a girl not a boy?
Is it really that much of your business?
Your discomfort should moderate joy?

You think that the world doesn't matter?
Cause the water polluted in haste
May drip a few coins in your wallet
And ruin the world to a waste.

Do you think your religion is all that?
Creation created for you?
That only your life is of value?
That others should burn but not you?

Can't you see that people are hungry?
Have you blocked them all out of your view?
As you pile your plate a bit higher
And think you need more as you chew.

Celebrate Me?

I know what you are thinking
And how you let it grow
The seeds of hate inside yourself
The darkness that you sow
Should you celebrate me now?
Should you expose what you know?

You are I are different
Me and you are not the same
I have flaws and you have faults
I heard you left before I came
Could you celebrate me now?
Could you call me by my name?

The battles I have been through
And the ones that you have seen
Different journeys, different lands
Dirtied sinners grubbied clean
Would you celebrate me now?
Would you call me what you mean?

One thousand miles you never walked
A road you never had to take
A place you never visited
Endless choices not to make
Will you celebrate me now?
Will you make foundations shake?

Eulogy for Change

If I heard you were dead I would not mourn.
   I would not mourn for you.
Your ideas and actions and attitudes are abhorrent to
     me.
The way you crashed through life,
The way you sat in your tower,
The way you looked down from your pinnacle.
The way you protected only those in your intimate
    circle
Whose experience of the world
Was your experience of the world.
I would remember you but I would not mourn.

Except
I would mourn the fact that you missed the rest.
You missed the mess; you missed the world!
That
If you had just
   Thought or noticed
      or listened or seen
         or looked or wondered or cared
   Or used just a shred of empathy or compassion,
You
could have changed this world for the better.
I believe you could
But you didn't and you wouldn't
But you could.

If I heard you were dead
   I would not mourn.

Your News

I heard your news with sorrow and the tears welled in my eyes.
I felt your pain and watched you bravely stifling your cries.
I saw the shock upon your face and furrows on your brow
And in your silence ask yourself "What should I do now?"
Ineffectually, I hang around and try to be of use.
Words all fail and actions stalled with nothing to produce.
A big and useless lump of clay, a straw hat on a rainy day
A kid that wants to run away, urged overwhelmingly to stay.
A bumpy journey lays ahead, rough roads and rougher seas.
I'm no guide or wiseman to help at times like these
But I will stay beside you love, as long as you have need.
No expectation nor resolve on that we are agreed.
Just company, and shoulders set to darkness we proceed
And when we're through, a promise just to quietly recede.

When We Part

When we part, I will recall only a handful of memories
From the hundreds and thousands of moments together.
When we part, I will have forgotten so much
That happened between us;
A handful of memories that slip and run
Through my fingers like sand.
Leaving dusty remains of happy days,
Sad times, intimate love, and public triumphs.
Precious images etched in my mind,
Fabled stories told and retold,
Familiar patterns, daily chores,
Warm smiles, wet tears.
Gathering dust,
Blowing away.
When we part, I will recall only a handful of memories,
From the hundreds and thousands of moments together.
When we part,
I will reach out and touch those few moments I recall
And hold them and cherish them,
Tug at them, caress them and encourage them
And find more
Tumbling out in recollection.
Blowing dust off the remnants of happy days,
Sad times, intimate love and public triumphs.
Trace the precious images etched in my mind,
Retell the fabled stories,
Blowing away gathering dust.
When we part, I will recall only a handful of memories
From the hundreds and thousands and millions of
        moments together.
Each a precious key unlocking more.

Gone Away

All the rooms that you don't enter
All the words you do not say
All the dreams you didn't finish
All the days you've gone away

All the hopes we had together
All the plans to fill each day
All the nights with one another
All the time you've gone away

All the years you won't be part of
All the games that we won't play
All the memories I must cling to
All our futures gone away

All the strength I have to muster
As I say goodbye today
All my heart in broken pieces
Now you've left and gone away

Poems of Dark Days

Passionless

There is no passion within me
There's nothing to stir up my soul
There is no feeling engaging
Or something I need to feel whole

There is no shining endeavor
There's nothing, no beacon of light
There is no quest to embark on
Or something to seek out with might

There is no goal I'm perusing
There nothing ambitious to reach
There is no deep joyful moment
But something continues to leach

The person I hoped that I would be
The success the triumph, my friend
There's a glimmer of hope left within me
Of the things I may start but can't end

Grey Wave

Grey waves on the horizon and a feeling in my soul
My weary aching body is re-falling down this hole
I think I have escaped it but the tide comes back again
And the rising flood of failing round me takes me back to
      when
I made it all go wrong before and how I messed it up
I drank it all, refilled again and drained each sickened cup
I don't know if I have the strength to carry on alone
I move my hat, I move my head, I move my heart and
      home
And the person deep within me still is always by my side
Tallying my failures and the times I should have died
Escaping grey waves, liquid offers momentary cheer
Must pull up and must stay dry and pull tomorrow near

Talisman

Keep me safe! On this I pray
With hand on heart, tucked safe away
Keep me near within thy grasp
In living moments' dying gasp
Keep me whole, while breaking down
With shattering dream or fracturing crown
Keep me free when I am chained
Unfairly caught and nearly drained
Keep the daytime, keep the night
Keep tomorrow keep the fight

Falling

Expecting the worst and telling the stories in my head
To myself, about myself and against myself
All the different horrific outcomes of situations and times
All those moments, argument and insanities
Times I failed, was abandoned and left alone.
Punished by circumstances
Devolved brain of my making
Session timed out due to inactivity
Heartless cruel imagination, seeking revenge
Or just inflicting punishment
Self-loathing inner monologues
Ruling my dream-space and
Conquering hope with depression
And fear

Love Me

Love me, love me, love me more,
Today, tomorrow, never score,
Or feed obsession, bang my head,
Spin me round and leave me dead.
I wasn't sure, I did not know.
I never knew how far to go.
Which part is right, or part is wrong;
The truth in stories, rhyme and song.
Tiny specks from long ago
From distant tales of love and woe
And life and loss and love and hymn,
When some succeed or never win.
Which way to go or path to choose
To make it right or really lose.
Love me, love me, love me more
Today, tomorrow ever more.
Love me, love me, love me more
Today, tomorrow never more.

Mirror Image

Sometimes I can see I'm quite handsome
Other times I'm as ugly as sin.
The same mirror tells me different stories
Dependent on which me looks in.
I think that the glass may be broken
Or the settings should all be reset
I think that it may have been warping
Or maybe I'm warped in my head.

Night Terrors

I have to write some words down here before this day is
     done
I must express these thoughts of mine before the rising sun
I must engage before I sleep, these words within my head
I have to let them leave my brain before I go to bed
I have to write these words out though their meaning isn't
     clear
I must aside my doubts all put and swallow down my fear
I mustn't fall asleep just yet though weary are my eyes
I couldn't know the good from bad the truth from wicked lies
I couldn't understand the falling danger that I'm in
I mustn't let the terror back I mustn't let it win
But what's the use and what's the hope when drowsiness
     arrives
While sinking into madness of these sleeping nightmare lives

Subjunctive Mood

If I were a workaholic
Imagine how much I'd get done
Think of the projects I'd finished
Instead I just sit on my bum

If I were a workaholic
Think of the things I'd complete
Picture the stuff I'd accomplish
Instead I'm accepting defeat

If I were a gymaholic
Imagine the weights I could lift
Picture my rippling muscles
Instead of the weight I can't shift

Instead, I'm a chocaholic
And I used to drink too much wine
So, I'll be a bit careful with pressure
And in balance, I'm sure I'm just fine

Just like the movies

Can I have just the special moments
Only the highs and lows?
Can I have just the production numbers
Only the joys and woes?
Can I have just the big set pieces
Expansive scenes and lots?
Can I have just the romantic moments
Extensive twists and plots?
Can't I leave out the daily grind
Or just montage away?
Can't I just skip the boring bits
And liven up this day?

The Epic Poem

Today I will write my epic poem
It will be long with many verses

Today I won't write my epic poem
It ended too soon, call out the hearses.

Looking Busy

This is a time to start writing
To flurry my fingers on keys
To open a Word or an Excel
And type lot of words up like these

Just in case someone is looking
Or paying attention to me
I tippitty tap on my keyboard
Inertia replaced with busy

I'm making my face look quite pensive
And focus my eyes on a screen
As I concentrate hard on this project
And look just how busy I've been

And so, I can carry on typing
Pretending but making it real
The art of the fake till you make it
Is starting to have an appeal

Now is a moment for speeding
And sentences flowing right here
A full screen and making a word count
Has made my next poem appear

Yup

Well, life is just a bunch of copying mechanisms
Life is just a bunch of coping mechanisms
This life is just a bunch of coping mechanisms
And I don't know how to get through

Cause life is just a bunch of trials and tribulations
Life is just a bunch of trials and tribulations
This life is just a bunch of trials and tribulations
And I don't know why I should go through

This road's a bumpy, rocky, dusty destination
This road's a bumpy, rocky, dusty destination
Well, this road's a bumpy, rocky, dusty destination
And I don't know how long I'll go through

My love's can't live with you without you situation
My love's can't live with you without you situation
Yup, my love's can't live with you without you
          situation
But please just be there when I'm home

We're gone tomorrow but today we just kept waiting
We're gone tomorrow but today we just kept waiting
We're gone tomorrow but today we just kept waiting
Yeah, ... that our life and all

ABOUT THE AUTHOR

Simon Mathis was born in London, England. He trained as a professional dancer, singer and actor but after a few years of performing and enjoying living in different places around the world he decided to preserve his knee joints. Simon has worked in corporate spaces as an administrative professional for the past seventeen years, which is a horrifying realization but is much more stable if far less enjoyable. He met his American husband Paul in Paris, France by chance, fate, or just good fortune, and emigrated to the USA in 2015 when they got married. He credits his wonderful parents, Adele and Norman, for his work ethic, people skills and his empathy. He misses his sister Rebecca and his friends, especially Lex, Jenny, Davis and Paul (a different Paul) who are still in the UK and he loves them all dearly. Currently, Simon works in NYC and his home is in the Catskills Mountains in upstate New York with Paul and his two cats Merlin & Tallulah. He has a B.A. in History and an M.S. in Human Resources Management.

Cats are weird, furry and scratchy hobgoblins that run up and down the stairs during the night. They are beautiful, delightful, annoying and troublesome. If you don't have cats, I highly recommend you get some. Sx

40th Birthday Portrait of Simon Mathis
Painted by his incredibly talented friend,
Zachary Ares, 2022